AF126351

BOOK ANALYSIS

By Jim Hilton

Sanctuary

BY WILLIAM FAULKNER

Bright
≡Summaries.com

WILLIAM FAULKNER

AMERICAN WRITER

- **Born in New Albany, Mississippi in 1897.**
- **Died in Byhalia, Mississippi in 1962.**
- **Notable works:**
  - *The Sound and the Fury* (1929), novel
  - *As I Lay Dying* (1930), novel
  - *Absalom, Absalom!* (1936), novel

Born William Cuthbert Falkner (the correct spelling of his family name), the winner of the 1949 Nobel Prize in Literature grew up in a literary family while also learning to ride horses, hunt and fish. His strongest influences were his mother, who encouraged him to read and draw, and his nanny Caroline Barr.

He did not graduate from high school, and then managed to enlist in the Canadian Royal Airforce by pretending to be British, but World War I ended before he flew any active missions, which did not stop him from adopting the persona (and the uniform) of an RAF pilot when he returned to Mississippi.

Prior to 1926, when his debut novel *Soldiers' Pay* was published, he wrote mainly poetry and absorbed the work of modernists such as the British-American poet T.S Elliot (1888-1965) and the Irish novelist James Joyce (1882-1941). He was advised by the American writer Sherwood Anderson (1876-1941) to write stories based on the rural Mississippi countryside that included his home town of Oxford, advice which resulted in his creation of the fictional Yoknapatawpha County, which became the setting for the majority of his novels.

When he published the controversial novel *Sanctuary* in 1931, it sold well and aroused interest in his earlier novels such as *The Sound and the Fury* (1929). This book, and his novels published during the 1930s, such as *Light in August* (1932) and *Absalom, Absalom!* (1936), are usually considered his best work, and have attracted more analyses and criticism than any other 20th century writer, due to his dense, challenging text full of symbolism, linguistic experimentation and deeply flawed characters.

Faulkner continued to write on difficult themes such as race, death and sexuality through the 1940s and 1950s. He died from thrombosis developed after a riding accident in 1962.

SANCTUARY

A DESPERATELY GRIM TALE OF EVIL AND INJUSTICE IN THE DEEP SOUTH

Content Warning: *Rape, sexual violence, sexual enslavement*

In dealing with the themes and content of Faulkner's novel, this study guide contains descriptions that some readers may find distressing.

- **Genre:** novel
- **Reference edition:** Faulkner, W. (2011) *Sanctuary.* London: Vintage.
- **1ˢᵗ edition:** 1931
- **Themes:** rape, evil, law, justice, lust, gender, the Deep South

William Faulkner completed his first manuscript of *Sanctuary* in 1929, but was informed by his publisher that the story was too lurid for publication. Nonetheless, Faulkner kept editing and adjusting, and the novel was published by Jonathan Cape in 1931. In 1933, a film adaptation titled *The Story of Temple Drake* was released, and although the explicit content was watered down, it remained highly controversial. Another film version, titled *Sanctuary* and directed by Tony Richardson (English filmmaker, 1928-1991), was released in 1961. This second version brought in elements from Faulkner's 1951 sequel to *Sanctuary, Requiem for a Nun*.

Having abandoned his wife and step-daughter, lawyer Horace Benbow is in need of a project to take his mind off things. Unfortunately for him, the case that lands in his lap is an unwinnable one: a twisted tale of rape and murder among the criminal underclass of Faulkner's fictional Yoknapatawpha County. The young debutante, Temple Drake – the daughter of a judge – is another upper-class outsider, with no business among ragged moonshiners and their common-law wives. It is only through a mean stroke of fate that she ends up trapped, kidnapped and enslaved by the murderous booze-runner, Popeye – surely one of Faulkner's vilest creations. Faulkner was reputed to have thought of *Sanctuary* as his potboiler, but in reality it reads like a kind of anti-thriller. Each vividly drawn location, from the moonshiners' hideout to Miss Reba's brothel in Memphis, feels designed to make the reader feel trapped and breathless – smothered by the Southern climate, and the thick, nauseating vapours of violence and lust.

SUMMARY

CHAPTERS I-IV

While hitchhiking from Kinston to Jefferson, lawyer Horace Benbow is accosted by Popeye – a sinister criminal who is currently staying at Lee Goodwin's moonshine distillery. Popeye brings Benbow to Goodwin's house, and Benbow is treated to dinner and a sample of the produce. Benbow talks drunkenly about his wife and step-daughter, who he has left for good. He is struck by Lee Goodwin's common-law wife, Ruby Lamar, who used to work as a streetwalker, and has a young sickly infant.

The next afternoon, Benbow has reached his sister Narcissa's house, just outside Jefferson. He meets the young bachelor Gowan Stevens, a graduate from Virginia who has been courting Narcissa. That same night, Gowan Stevens is taking a young lady student at Ole Miss, Temple Drake, to a dance. The dance finishes and he drops her off, after making a plan to go with her to the baseball the next day on an early train.

Driving back, Gowan picks up some local lads who advise him where to procure some alcohol, and the four of them go out to Lee Goodwin's.

The next morning, Gowan wakes up in his car – having passed out after last night's binge. He has missed the train, but manages to catch up with it at the next station, where Temple disembarks – highly unimpressed at Gowan's condition. He commits to getting them to the game by car, but also decides to drop by Goodwin's again to pick up more alcohol. Coming towards the house, Gowan, still somewhat drunk, crashes into a tree that lies across the road. Luckily neither of them are injured.

CHAPTERS V-IX

Popeye and Tommy, Goodwin's mentally-impaired helper, are nearby when the crash happens, and they escort Gowan and Temple up to the house. Temple is immediately alarmed by the atmosphere of the place, and Ruby Lamar warns her to leave before nightfall, and cruelly upbraids her for her naivety and fickleness. Gowan is busy getting drunk again. Lee Goodwin and another colleague, Van, arrive back at the house, and Van makes unpleasant advances towards Temple at dinner. Van and Gowan have a brief tussle, while Goodwin attempts to make peace. By now it is nighttime, and Temple takes refuge in a guest room. Gowan has passed out drunk and the men barge in, throwing him on the bed. Under the watch of Ruby Lamar and Tommy, Temple remains safe for now, as the men head out to make a delivery. Under the cover of darkness, Ruby takes Temple out to the grain barn, where she spends the night guarding her.

CHAPTERS X-XIV

The next morning, Gowan – still a bit drunk – goes to dispatch a car for the two of them, but decides he cannot face Temple again after last night. He sends the car back for her, and carries on to town by himself. Although it is daylight, Temple realises that she is still in danger, and that Goodwin and Popeye both mean her harm. Tommy, who is instinctively sympathetic towards her, guards the door of the barn where she is still hiding, but Popeye sneaks in through the back and shoots him in the head with his pistol, killing him. Popeye then proceeds to rape Temple with a corncob. Walking back to the house from the spring, Ruby sees Popeye driving away in his car with Temple, her face "like a small, dead-coloured mask", in the passenger seat beside him (p. 69).

CHAPTERS XV-XX

After a thorough dressing-down from his sister, Horace Benbow has moved into their old childhood home in town. Lee Goodwin has been arrested for Tommy's murder, but fearing reprisals from Popeye, is refusing to cooperate with the police or to offer an alternative version of events. Benbow has taken Goodwin on as a client, and puts Ruby Lamar and the baby up at a hotel (after Narcissa forbids him from letting her stay at their old childhood house). Benbow urges Goodwin to at least give him a full run-down of what happened, but Goodwin stolidly refuses. Finally Ruby gives in and tells Benbow of Temple's presence at the house that night.

Leaving Goodwin's distillery, Popeye drives Temple to Memphis, where he installs her in a brothel run by a sentimental, asthmatic madam, Miss Reba, who summons a doctor to see to

Temple's wounds. Miss Reba is a steady drinker, and under her care, Temple begins to pick up the habit. Temple has effectively been sex trafficked. Despite Miss Reba's friendliness and the comfort of the accommodation, Temple's room is really a prison, and she is held there at Popeye's convenience.

Benbow travels to Ole Miss to enquire about Temple, but learns only that she has suspended her studies. On the train back, he meets a craven state senator, Clarence Snopes, who reports that Temple's "paw sent her up north somewhere" (p. 120). When Benbow arrives back in Jefferson, he learns that a local committee of women have forced the local hotelier to evict Ruby Lamar. Benbow has another argument with his sister about his involvement in the case.

CHAPTERS XXI-XXIII

The senator, Clarence Snopes, meets his cousin at Miss Reba's brothel in Memphis, and there learns of Temple Drake's fate. Benbow finally manages to find new accommodation for Ruby and the baby: a "ramshackle house" on the edge of town belonging to a "half-crazed white woman" and manufacturer of spells (p. 136). Snopes contacts Benbow and clumsily makes it clear that he will reveal Temple's location for a bribe, and Benbow agrees. Benbow travels to Memphis and Miss Reba allows him to speak with Temple, who gives him her account of the events of that night and the morning after. Benbow then makes his way back to Jefferson, deeply shaken.

CHAPTERS XXIV-XXV

Temple bribes Miss Reba's servant, Minnie, ten dollars to let her out quickly to make a telephone call. Later, seeming as if she is about to escape, Temple furtively leaves the bordello, but is caught by Popeye and forced into his car. It is only now that the exact nature of Popeye's abuse begins to become clear. We learn that Popeye apparently cannot perform penetrative sex, and that he has been forcing a local gangster, Red, to rape Temple, while he watches. Temple, meanwhile, has started to develop feelings for Red. Now Popeye drives her to a roadhouse called the Grotto for some kind of showdown between the three of them. In a moment away from Popeye, Temple tries to seduce Red, but he puts her off. She is finally escorted out by some of Popeye's henchmen, who take her back to the brothel, passing Popeye, who is parked in his car, waiting for Red to leave.

An extended comic sequence ensues, over which we learn that Red has been shot and killed by Popeye, who has escaped. Red's funeral becomes a punch-up between drunk mourners, while Miss Reba and two of her friends drown their woes and shake their heads at Popeye's deviant sexual practices.

CHAPTERS XXVI-XXXI

Benbow's sister Narcissa visits the prosecuting lawyer, District Attorney Eustace Graham, asking him to win the case as quickly as possible. Benbow, meanwhile, now knowing the truth and knowing Temple's location in Memphis, believes he can get Goodwin off. At court, Temple is called to the stand. D.A. Graham presents the court with the blood-stained corncob, which has been retrieved from the barn, and provocatively suggests "that this is no longer a matter for the hangman, but for a bonfire of gasoline" (p. 195). Under examination by Graham, Temple gives false testimony that it was Goodwin that shot Tommy, and Goodwin who committed the rape. At the conclusion of her testimony, Temple's father comes to the stand and leads her from the court. The jury find Goodwin guilty after only "eight minutes" (p. 200). Benbow is disconsolate at the outcome of the trial and later that night wanders into the centre of Jefferson. He discovers Goodwin being lynched by an angry mob, and only narrowly escapes the same fate. Defeated and tired, Benbow returns to his wife and step-daughter in Kinston.

Popeye has flown the state, but is arrested in Birmingham, Alabama on the way to visit his mother. Ironically, the charge is for a murder that Popeye did not in fact commit. Nonetheless, he is apathetic towards the whole process and has no interest whatsoever in defending himself. We learn some sparse details of his traumatic and neglected childhood, and he is executed for the murder.

The novel ends with Temple and her father sitting in the Luxembourg Gardens in Paris at dusk. She studies her face in her compact: "a face in miniature sullen and discontented and sad" (p. 219).

CHARACTER STUDY

TEMPLE DRAKE

Temple Drake is a 17-year-old student at Ole Miss, and the daughter of a judge. She is quite wild for her age, regularly dating students at the weekends and town boys during the week. One of her regular escorts, the pompous alcoholic Gowan Stevens, is alarmed to discover her name scrawled on a bathroom stall in town. Temple is effectively passed between men throughout the novel: from Gowan's boozed inefficacy to Popeye's vilely abusive control, and finally back into the caring arms of her father. It is a sad progress. She escapes her literal imprisonment and sex slavery, but her supposed freedom in fact only resembles another mode of patriarchal control.

POPEYE

Popeye is an idiosyncratic and perverted villain, and the rest of the characters around him repeatedly comment on his strangeness. He has little interest in storytelling, or gambling or drinking or any of the usual pastimes of the criminal. We later learn that his refusal to touch alcohol is actually a medical necessity. We also learn about his childhood: his absentee father, his grandmother who burned down their house and his mother who went mad with it all. Faulkner gives us this explanation for his condition, for there is no excuse nor possibility of redemption in the fact. He is a hopelessly damaged creature and he seemingly cannot but damage others around him.

HORACE BENBOW

Horace Benbow is the character we are asked to identify with most. His tiredness in the face of the world's evil most closely resembles our response as readers – we who may at times feel like shutting the book and leaving it shut. Benbow is no hero, however, and his motives are far from pure. He has left his wife and step-daughter, seemingly due to his own conflicted passions concerning the young girl. During his stay in Jefferson, Benbow manages to transfer his attentions to Ruby Lamar. He pours all of his efforts as a lawyer into releasing Lamar's common-law husband from a false charge, insisting at regular intervals on his purely moral intentions and each time leaving us more and more in doubt.

RUBY LAMAR

Ruby Lamar is Lee Goodwin's common-law wife. Although only in her early 20s, she has undergone a world of adversity, and stuck by Lee through thick and thin – well past the point of his deserving. Unlike Temple, who as a student may freely throw herself into joviality, dances and swift flings, Ruby has had to learn the mainstays of female existence on a tough society's fringes: namely sex, cooking and child-rearing. Ruby's stint as a sex-worker makes her a social pariah in Jefferson, and Horace's involvement with her is a constant source of anxiety to his sister Narcissa.

MISS REBA

Miss Reba provides some of the only (and much-welcomed) comic relief in the novel. She is a larger-than-life personality: a whirlwind of a woman, asthmatic (forever heaving up and down stairs), forceful, caring and also deeply sentimental. Between bouts of day-drinking, she often collapses into a tipsy fit of tears at the thought of her dead husband, proclaiming to anyone who is near her that "For eleven years we was like two doves" (p. 176). She has two small dogs named Miss Reba and Mr Binford (after her and her late husband) who are constantly fawning and yapping, and are regularly delivered a swift kick by her as they flail around her legs.

ANALYSIS

VIOLENCE, SENSATIONALISM AND THE MOVIES

Like so many 20th century American writers, William Faulkner struggled to make a living from his novels alone, and throughout his career he turned to the Hollywood film studios as a source of income. In 1932 he signed a contract with MGM as a screenwriter, and for the next two decades he would find occasional work writing movies. His most famous credit was for Howard Hawks' (American filmmaker, 1896-1977) celebrated film *The Big Sleep* (1946) starring Humphrey Bogart (American actor, 1899-1957) and Lauren Bacall (American actor, 1924-2014) – adapted from the great Raymond Chandler (American writer, 1888-1959) novel of the same name. Along with F. Scott Fitzgerald (American writer, 1896-1940), another great novelist who served an unhappy term in Hollywood penning movies, Faulkner has become a romantic paradigm of the frustrated, booze-soaked artist, peddling away his genius in a movie industry that privileged action over substance and box-office returns over artistic merit. The Coen Brothers' (American filmmakers Joel, born in 1954–, and Ethan, born in 1957) period drama film *Barton Fink* (1991) even features John Mahoney (English actor, 1940-2018) as an alcoholic Southern screenwriter, clearly modelled on Faulkner.

The unprecedented industrial development of Hollywood in early 20th century America, and its new role in the socio-economic existence of American writers, makes it an important lens through which to view most novels of the period (even novels which, on the surface, do not seem to have any explicit links to cinema). *Sanctuary* was first published in 1931, and a Hollywood film adaptation – called *The Story of Temple Drake* – would be released as soon as 1933. Even though the filmmakers toned down the novel's graphic descriptions of violence, this pre-Code film caused a massive public outcry. *The Story of Temple* Drake in fact became a crucial movie in the ongoing public debate about moral decency in Hollywood films. Conservative political forces viewed it, as well as contemporary gangster films such as *Scarface* (1932), *Little Caesar* (1931) and *The Public Enemy* (1931), as dangerous and corrupting, and commentators argued that the glorification of violence on screen would draw people into the criminal lifestyles represented. Under this increasing pressure, from mid-1934 onwards, the film studios were forced to adhere to the Hays Code. This was a film production code that censored the extent of violence and sex that could be presented on screen (one of its most infamous strictures was that a filmed kiss could last no longer than 3 seconds).

The extent to which Faulkner thought of *Sanctuary* as his potboiler has been disputed by critics, and certainly it does not read like a thriller. The crimes presented are despicable, rather than exciting. There is murder, but there is no gun-play – no climactic car chases nor police standoffs. The action that there is, is ponderously slow and deeply disturbing. Popeye is uniquely anti-romantic as a villain, eliciting no sympathy from the reader nor any moments of character identification. Horace Benbow, meanwhile, is hardly a hero: he is hopelessly ineffectual, and his motives regarding Ruby and Goodwin stand in constant question.

So did Faulkner really write *Sanctuary* with movie royalties in mind? According to the above criteria, maybe not. And yet the extent of the violence he portrays, and particularly the sexual violence, feels self-consciously sensationalizing. Did he predict that the novel's gratuitousness would provide it with a wider platform? And if he did, should this affect how we read it?

SANCTUARY'S WOMEN

For a novel based in large part around a horrific rape, the victim – Temple Drake – does not get much of a say in the finished narrative. We spend a large part of the novel with her, but for most of that time, we feel as though we are on the outside: watching her terror, her powerlessness from our own powerless position as readers. The largest insight we get into her way of seeing things occurs during her conference with Benbow, where she describes the night she spent at the house, and how she lay on the bed, hiding from the men:

> "I was looking at my legs and I'd try to make like I was a boy. I was thinking about if I just was a boy and then I tried to make myself into one by thinking." (p. 148)

She then compares the thought to being in school, when you know an answer and try to mentally project your willingness to the teacher: "Call on me. Call on me. Call on me" (*ibid*.). Maybe the problem with Faulkner's portrayal of Temple, if there is a problem, is that she is so clearly and completely a child. She is so immature and has been so sheltered that she simply stands no chance against the awful predicament in which she finds herself – a scenario so hellish that even an adult could not necessarily escape.

A problem that modern readers might encounter on studying *Sanctuary* is the faint but gnawing implication that Temple is partly responsible for what happens to her: that because of her childishness and her naivety, she is a prime target, bringing down evil upon herself. Faulkner's principal mouthpiece for this opinion is in fact Ruby Lamar, a former sex-worker, who is only a bit older than Temple but has seen far more of life's hardships. On the night they meet, she scolds Temple roughly: "I know your sort. I've seen them. All running, but not too fast" (p. 40). Ruby is bitterly torn between concern, wanting Temple to leave before dark, and wrath at her fickle helplessness. For Ruby, class distinctions undermine her instinctive female solidarity. She is enraged that Temple, so clearly a student, moneyed and respectable – indeed a judge's daughter – should let herself fall into a so clearly dangerous situation. It is almost enough to make Ruby actively wish her harm, and yet not quite. When the time comes, Ruby does her best to protect the younger girl.

The novel's other main inter-female conflict is between Ruby and Horace Benbow's sister Narcissa, even though the two characters never meet face-to-face. Benbow and Narcissa are well-off, respected people, and as Narcissa keeps telling her brother, it is completely inappropriate that he be seen in town consorting with a prostitute. Benbow bows to his sister's stricter demands, not letting Ruby stay in their childhood home for instance, but he will not cut off contact with Ruby completely, and indeed he sees Goodwin's case through to the bitter end. For most of the novel, Narcissa's attitude strikes Horace and the reader as hopelessly small-minded and selfish. Even her name seems to recall that character from Greek mythology,

Narcissus, who fell in love with his own reflection and drowned. But in a conversation between Horace and Narcissa, Faulkner cleverly and poignantly shifts focus to the gendered nature of social space and opportunity in the Deep South. Narcissa tells her brother:

> "I don't care where you live. The question is, where I live. I live here, in this town. I'll have to stay here. But you're a man. It doesn't matter to you. You can go away. [...] This is my home, where I must spend the rest of my life." (p. 125)

It is easy for Horace Benbow as a man to play the Good Samaritan and to close his ears to the idle gossips of the town, but this invulnerability is tied into his identity. Sure enough, at the novel's end, he returns home to his wife in Kinston, while Narcissa of course stays on in Jefferson: caught, in her own way, like Ruby and Temple.

FURTHER REFLECTION

SOME QUESTIONS TO THINK ABOUT...

- While Popeye successively avoids conviction for Tommy's murder and Temple's rape, he is ultimately sentenced to execution for another murder – one he did not actually commit. What might Faulkner be saying about justice here?
- *Sanctuary* often feels uncompromising and even gratuitous. Does art have a responsibility to be redeeming in some way, or is there a greater responsibility to present the true evils of the world?
- Towards the end of the novel, the lousy state senator Clarence Snopes launches into an openly anti-Semitic diatribe concerning a Jewish lawyer. Why might Faulkner be concerned about anti-Semitic prejudice in the early 1930s?
- Amongst the novel's largely serious and difficult themes and content, there are certain moments of light relief: moments with Miss

Reba and her friends, Red's funeral and Virgil Snopes' stay in the brothel. Do these moments work, and should comedy sit so closely next to tragedy?

- The Deep South is well-known as a centre of religious conservatism and fast-held belief, yet religion hardly seems to appear at all in *Sanctuary*. Why might this be?
- Faulkner once reputedly called *Sanctuary* his "potboiler". Can we take this claim seriously? Explain your answer.

We want to hear from you!
Leave a comment on your online library
and share your favourite books on social media!

FURTHER READING

REFERENCE EDITION

- Faulkner, W. (2011) *Sanctuary*. London: Vintage.

ADAPTATIONS

- *The Story of Temple Drake*. (1933) [Film]. Stephen Roberts. Dir. United States: Paramount Pictures.
- *Sanctuary*. (1961) [Film]. Tony Richardson. Dir. United States: 20th Century Fox.

MORE FROM BRIGHTSUMMARIES.COM

- Reading guide – *As I Lay Dying* by William Faulkner.
- Reading guide – *Light in August* by William Faulkner.
- Reading guide – *The Sound and the Fury* by William Faulkner.
- Reading guide – *The Wishing Tree* by William Faulker.

www.brightsummaries.com

Ebook EAN: 9782808019484

Paperback EAN: 9782808019491

Legal Deposit: D/2019/12603/141

Cover: © Primento

Digital conception by Primento, the digital partner of publishers.